Prickles

by Catherine W. Weiser

Catherine W. Weiser

10/09/16

Illustrator: Grace G. Sisco

Editors: Debby Milledge and Jackie Milledge

Research Assistant: David Robles

ISBN: 978-1-937260-57-6

Sleepytown Press

www.sleepytownpress.com

Prickles is dedicated to:

My new great great nephews: Andrew Timothy Johnson
                                               Ryan Wade Appleby

My best fan: Beau Mims

My young friends: Rhett Walters
                                               Lake Walters
                                                Karianne Amis
                                                Landon Amis
                                                Mallory McLaurin Amis

Hello! Is someone there? I can hear you breathing, but I cannot see you because I was born blind. This makes me very sad. I feel better now because my mother gave me a pacifier. I love my "pacie!"

Please do not worry about me being blind. I have a thick covering over my eyes just like baby kittens do when they are born. This covering goes away after five to seven days. I definitely see better at night, although my eyesight stays very weak all my life. I am glad that I can see fairly well now because I am looking for a friend to play with me.

Ouch

Quill

Itsy-Bitsy

Prickles

Pokey

Sharp

Four boys and one girl were born at the same time I was born. My mother named me Prickles. My brothers are named Ouch, Quill, Pokey, and Sharp. My sister's name is Itsy-Bitsy. I love my brothers and sister. We are very active and play together every day. They are nice to me when I am lonely, but I would have more fun if I had one best friend.

Do you know what kind of animal I am? I am a boy hedgehog. I don't know why I am called a hedgehog. Some people call me a hog-let. Maybe they call me a hedgehog because I like to run under the hedges and hide. I don't look like a hog, but I do make pig-like grunts which sound like "Oink, Oink." If I came out from under the hedges, I would probably get stuck in the mud near this pig!

I am not happy when people call me a hog because hogs eat a lot of food. I eat very little food, but I do like beetles, caterpillars, earthworms, mushrooms, grass roots, snake eggs, and bird eggs. I like to root through the grasses and hedges to find my food. I also like to chew on wood and roots. I am allergic to milk, so I must be very careful not to drink it. The earthworm I am eating is hard to chew. It wiggles too much!

I was born hairless, but my quills began to grow about thirty-six hours after I was born. The quills were very soft at first but became more hard and prickly later. Wait a minute! I think I just saw another hedgehog. I wonder if it is a boy or a girl hedgehog.

I grow almost 5,000 quills on my body. Each quill lasts about a year before it drops off and is replaced with a new quill. Hidden under my quills can be up to five hundred fleas or lice, but they rarely bite humans. If you have a back-scratcher, I would like to borrow it, but it would be better if I had a friend to scratch my back.

When I become an adult hedgehog, I am about the size of a golf ball. My quills look dangerous, but they are not sharp and will rarely hurt you if you hold me. If your dad plays golf, I hope he will not mistake me for the golf ball and try to use me to shoot a hole-in-one! Wait a minute! Is that a girl hedge-hog in my golf cart?

My lifespan is up to six years, so I try to protect myself from my enemies, such as owls, ferrets, foxes, and wolves. These enemies like to eat meat. If my enemies come near me, I curl into a ball and look like a large roly-poly. Wait a minute! Do you think that fox looks suspicious? I think he looks like he needs something to eat. It's time for me to protect myself!

Indian
Hedgehog

Egyptian
Hedgehog

Desert
Hedgehog

There are seventeen types of hedgehogs
Some of the types are the desert hedgehog, the Egyptian hedgehog, the Indian
hedgehog, and the four-toed hedgehog. I
am an African pygmy hedgehog. Isn't the
Egyptian hedgehog beautiful? I wonder if
she would be my friend?

Some fun facts about me are that I can run over six feet per second, which is obviously faster than a turtle. I love to take a bath and can float on my back in water. I can be brown, black, beige, gray or even albino (white). I am a light brown color with a beige-colored chest. I think I am handsome!

Hedgehogs are mentioned in many books and stories. A writer named Shakespeare mentioned me in two of his plays, *The Tempest* and *A Midsummer Night's Dream*. He called me a thorny hedgehog and an urchin. An urchin means an unkempt child. I am not a child, and I keep myself neat and clean!

My question for you is this:

Would you like to have a hedgehog or not? That is the question.

Hedgehogs are solitary animals, but two girls can live in the same cage. would like to have a friend in my cage, but because I am a boy, I must live alone. I really would like to have a friend that is a boy, or even a girlfriend!

A girl hedgehog can have babies when she is one year old. Most baby hedgehogs are born in June and July. The average litter size is four or five babies Young hedgehogs leave the nest when they are three or four weeks old to go foraging for food under hedges and around tree roots. After ten days of foraging, the young will leave their mother and wander off on their own. I miss my mother very much, but I still see her and my brothers and sister over in the woods near my burrow. All my brothers and sister have families now.

Hedgehogs in Europe, on the other side of the world, hibernate. They are not really asleep; instead, their body temperature drops, and they enter a state of inactivity. This allows them to save a lot of energy. I get tired in cold weather, so I am glad to have a period of rest, but I really don't hibernate like the European hedgehogs.

If you would like to see if you have hedgehogs around your house, you can tell if they leave tracks. Put a large piece of light-colored plastic on the ground near a bush or hedge. Add large rocks to each corner of the plastic so it will not blow away. Place a bowl of food (bait) in the center of the plastic. You can use worms or soft vegetables, like celery or lettuce, for food. Pour ink around the bowl. (Your mother or father will need to buy the ink for you at the store). When the hedgehog comes to feed, it will step in the ink and leave a trail of footprints as it runs away. I know what you are thinking: other critters may leave footprints also. A hedgehog's footprints look like this:

Wouldn't it be wonderful if a hedgehog named Prickles came to eat!

There are many positive reasons to own a hedgehog.

1. Hedgehogs are quiet pets.

2. They are clean, and you only have to clean their cage once a week.

3. Hedgehogs that eat good food do not have a distinctive body odor.

4. They do not have dry skin like cats and dogs, so they are good pets for people with allergies.

5. They are not aggressive by nature.

6. They enjoy fresh food and water daily.

7. They do not require yearly shots.

There are negative reasons for owning a hedgehog.

1. Hedgehogs are prickly.

2. The average hedgehog is shy and nervous.

3. They are nocturnal animals, which means that they are awake for most of the night.

4. Hedgehogs may be grouchy.

5. Handle a hedgehog every day because it may take a long time for it to like you.

6. Hedgehogs have teeth and may bite you if they are scared.

7. Trips to the veterinarian may be costly if your pet is sick.

8. Hedgehogs will need at least one lice treatment during their lifetime.

Tips from: MF Critter Connection

I have finally found out who has been following me. A Yorkie puppy name
Teddy has been sneaking around behind me. He came running up to me one
day and licked my face. He has another hedgehog friend named Splinter. She
is a beautiful girl hedgehog. I saw her in my golf cart one day. Teddy intro-
duced her to me. I have good news: she is my new girlfriend. You will find
out more about my new friends in my next story. Goodbye! I'll see you soon!

Catherine W. Weiser lives in Jacksonville, AL, with her husband William. They have one daughter, Denise, and one son, Bill. Catherine and William have six granddaughters, and one of their granddaughters, Grace, is the illustrator of this book. Catherine is a motivational speaker and a retired elementary school teacher. She loves hedgehogs, especially the babies. Catherine has written two other books, *Searching For Rainey Hill*, published in 2013, and *What Color Is a Ladybug?*, published in 2014.

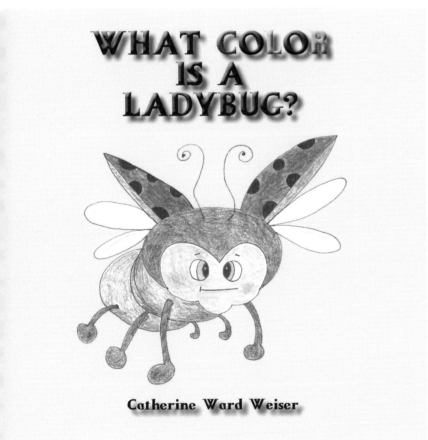

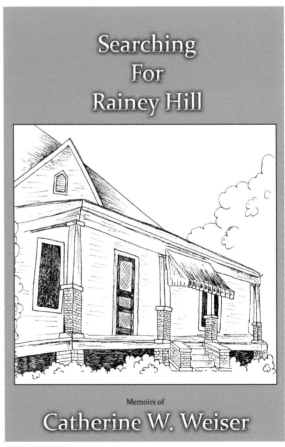

CPSIA information can be obtained at www.ICGtesting.com
Printed in the USA
LVIW01n0033020916
502724LV00002B/2